To:

_____

From:

Humbug, A Christmas Carol

Text © 2009 by Lee Baker

Illustrations © Lee Baker & Stephen Sobisky

www.humbugchristmas.com

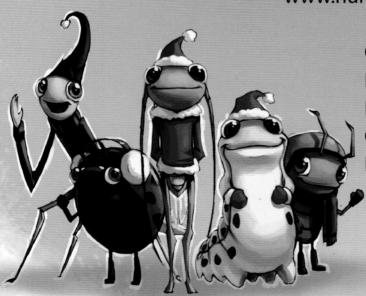

Composed in the United States of America

Printed in United States of America

Edited by Lee Baker

Creative Direction by Stephen Sobisky

Illustrations by Kienan Lafferty & Andrew Young

FIRST IMPRESSION 2009

ISBN   978-0-615-33839-2

To our families who continue to believe.

- L. B., S. S., K. L.

Humbug

A christmas carol

by Lee Baker

With a Foreword by Ebenezer Scrooge

Foreword:

To Whom It May Concern,

I have never seen a Humbug. I have never heard a Humbug hum. People can talk of fairy tales and fantastic magical creatures, but that does not make them real. Humbugs do not exist!

Sternly,
Ebenezer Scrooge

HumbuG

Winterton was a small frozen town nestled between two large mountains and hidden from the rest of the world. In Winterton, the weather was cold, the houses were cold, the food was cold, the people were cold and worst of all, love, kindness and joy had left with the belief in Christmas.

No person in Winterton had lived long enough to remember a Christmas. No one had seen Santa and gifts were never shared or exchanged. Cards were obsolete. In fact, the people rarely spoke to each other. They only opened their mouths when it was absolutely necessary and when they did, it was strictly business and if your business was not their business, you were left standing alone in the cold.

The Winterton railroad station was as frozen as the hearts of the people. An icy train pulled into the station, the people exited the train and without any noise or speaking they filtered their way out leaving a small young girl alone, sitting on her small suitcase. She was different. Her cheeks were rosy and her eyes bright. She smiled as she looked around at the large building then pulled a small box out of her pocket and opened it. Inside was a small green bug wearing a red and white hat.

 "I guess this is our new home," she said to the bug. The bug looked around, smiled and a slight hum came from his lips. "Of course you can," said the young girl with a smile. The bug's hum increased, he smiled again and flew from the young girl's hand.

   Mrs. Sleet, a stern woman with a sheet of frost covering her cheeks pushed through the front doors of the now barren station. She saw the young girl and coldly walked in a straight line directly toward her. The girl's warm smile was unrecognized and Mrs. Sleet took her hand, pulled her up, spun her around and dragged her across the wide open empty station and out the doors.

Humbug

Mayor Coldstone did not want to stay in his chair any longer when Mrs. Sleet opened his chilly office door. "She's not my business," Mayor Coldstone said in a cold tone.

"You are the mayor of Winterton and she is a new citizen," was the frigid response.

"You deal with her," he replied over his icy glasses.

"We have no room in the orphanage," replied Mrs. Sleet with a flat, arctic glare.

Mayor Coldstone looked at her intently, his frozen lips tightening. "Put her in the attic!" With that, Mayor Coldstone stood up and left the room.

Standing outside the door to his office was the cute, rosy-cheeked girl with a warm smile on her face. Mayor Coldstone stopped, looked down at the little girl, stepped to the side and walked out past her. Mrs. Sleet stalked out of the office and stopped in front of the girl. Her cold face firm with frustration, her purple lips opened to say, "You've been given a room." With that she grabbed the girl's hand and pulled her along.

Icicles hung from the buildings and frost lined the streets as Mrs. Sleet pulled the young cheerful girl toward the orphanage. Chester Chapman, a tall, ice-covered man sternly walked down the street holding the hand of a young stern boy. The girl saw the young boy and smiled brightly, "Hi, I'm Mimi."

The boy was shocked. What is she doing? He thought. Is she speaking to me? What is she doing with her face? It's moving in such strange ways. You see, the cold young boy had never seen a smile nor had he ever spoken with anyone on the street. He then, in desperation, did something he had never done in public -- he looked at his father.

Chester Chapman did not flinch, the ice frozen on his face remained smooth and his legs kept moving. The young boy turned back to the girl who continued to smile.

"I'm new here and maybe we can be friends," Mimi smiled with excitement and joy as Mrs. Sleet pulled her along down the street.

The boy was confused and quite frightened, but something inside him felt warm and bright. The sensation was new and he couldn't think straight, but he liked the feeling and Mimi was being pulled away. He had to act quickly if he was to act at all. His lips moved and twisted at first, but out came a word, almost a cough, "Charlie."

Mimi beamed and smiled even more, "I like you Charlie!" With those words Mimi was pulled through a door. Charlie continued down the street with his father, but the world had changed and become different somehow. Charlie looked into a window and practiced a grin. Icicles cracked and fell from his cheeks and inside came a warm feeling which was new to his little cold body.

The attic was cold, dark and scary. The floor was a sheet of ice which cracked as the hatch flew open. Mimi was pushed through the hole followed by a tattered blanket and pillow. "Excuse me, Mrs. Sleet?" said Mimi, looking down through the hole, "Did you know it's Christmas Eve?"

Mrs. Sleet was aghast that a child would speak directly to her and more irritated that the girl would speak of something so foreign. However, she did something that is rare in this wintery town; she looked at the child and spoke, "It is the 24th of December, yes. Christmas Eve, no! You cannot have an Eve of something that does not exist!" With that she coldly turned away.

"The Humbug will bring it," replied Mimi with a smile.

Mrs. Sleet was studious and had read every frost-covered book in the Winterton Library, however she had never heard of a Humbug. The chill of curiosity caught her and she stopped in her tracks. Without turning she questioned, "The Humbug?"

"Yes, I brought him with me and he's already making friends."

"Bah!" she protested and continued to walk.

"I can hear them already. There must be at least three."

Again she stopped, curiosity coming again, "What do Humbugs do?"

"They hum," Mimi replied with a giggle.

There was a long pause as Mrs. Sleet considered the thought, "And how will that bring Christmas?"

"The reindeer like it."

Humbug

"Ha!" laughed Mrs. Sleet with a shock. Her hand shot to her face and covered her mouth. She could not believe a laugh had snuck out. The feeling was odd, a tickle inside. She had never done it, never thought it, not once. But now it had happened, and she felt different somewhere inside.

"Humbugs make you laugh and smile," continued Mimi. "Everyone loves them." In a fluster and caught unaware, Mrs. Sleet was speechless and dared not turn around. Not knowing what to say she blurted out, "That's the most ridiculous thing I have ever heard," and she ran down the hall.

Around a corner she stopped and stood still. In the ice cold stillness she heard a slight sound. She listened more closely and the sound made a hum. A melody came through, although soft, it was clear. The sound was peaceful and joyful and warm. The frost on her cheeks melted and a smile slowly grew. Mrs. Sleet peeked around the corner and looked down the hall. Mimi was hanging from the hole in the ceiling, smiling and warm.

"It's beautiful isn't it?" said Mimi with delight.

"Why, yes…yes, it is," said Mrs. Sleet wrapped in a new emotion of cheer.

Then, in an uncomfortable realization that she was acting so strange, she forced the cold to return and spun around. "No!" she thought longer and colder and the frosty face returned, "It's senseless - not logical, not practical, not real. Who is making that music?!" She quickly marched down the hall, slid down the steps and forced open the door, determined to find the people humming so strangely.

The cold, numbing air refreshed Mrs. Sleet as her chill returned and frost again formed on her cheeks. She went through the village and questioned everyone in sight. The shivery shopkeeper denied any humming, then shut his door. The snappy seamstress stiffly suggested the bitter builder. The bitter builder kept building and bit his big lip. The polar postman gave a penetrating glare. The frigid fireman fought the accusation. The frozen farmer was fraught with frustration and refused to answer. Each villager approached was shocked with the suggestion, but stopped to listen after Mrs. Sleet had departed.

As each person listened an interesting thing happened. At first it was as quiet as quiet could be then a slight sound shimmered through the icy air. Listening more intently the melody became clear. It was a definite hum and it was everywhere. Something was happening that had never happened before. Each confused person asked if others could hear. For the first time in years people knocked on frost covered doors,

the cold doors were opened and questions were asked. Answers were given and people listened.
The humming was beautiful and started conversations. Icicles fell from cheeks and eyebrows as
people discussed the interesting sound. Occasionally a laugh sprang out as people interacted, but
when such a thing happened it was followed by, "Pardon me, please." Forgiveness was given and
each felt something change inside.

The town hall was filled with commotion and confusion. At the front of the room Mrs. Sleet stood with Mimi behind her. Mayor Coldstone entered, frozen and firm."Stop!" he shouted with a sharp, biting snap.

The hall was quiet, a crisp arctic silence. Mayor Coldstone walked forward and the villagers parted. The Mayor broke the silence. "I don't hear anything." The room broke into chaos as villagers protested. "Stop!" again was the silencing word from the icy Mayor. Quiet again. Mayor Coldstone listened and soon the chill silence was warmed with a beautiful hum. The Mayor listened and for a moment his scowl smoothed and an icicle cracked.

"Mayor," whispered Mrs. Sleet. "Do you hear it?"

"What is it?" questioned the Mayor.

"The Humbugs are humming for the reindeer," said Mimi as she stepped out from behind Mrs. Sleet with a coy grin.

The Mayor looked down at Mimi with wonderment, "Humbugs? Reindeer?"

"Yes, Humbugs attract Santa's reindeer."

"Santa?"

"Yes, they'll bring Christmas."

"Christmas?" coughed Mayor Coldstone. Then he laughed. Yes, you heard right, the Mayor actually laughed. Icicles showered from his face. He laughed a deep hearty laugh, a thing unheard of in Winterton. A wave of shocked looks spread through the cold hall. No one in Winterton had ever seen a deep hearty laugh – and this from the Mayor? He then rebutted, "Christmas? You think there will be a Christmas?"

Humbug

"Yes, I do," answered Mimi with a smile. You see, Mimi had learned that what you believe burns in your heart and when you believe in something it can change the world. When Mimi was born her parents were poor and she was left at the rickety doorstep of an old window washer.

The kind, frail, old man took in the baby and raised her as his own. What little he had was divided with the young child and as she grew up he taught her to believe. Mimi grew to love music and wanted to learn to sing, but in the old rickety shack she had nothing but bugs.

One night, with her heart burning inside, she asked one of the bugs to teach her a tune. The bug smiled, looked her in the eye and hummed the most beautiful tune she had ever heard. This Humbug became her best friend and comforted her with beautiful melodies of Christmas love as the old man passed away and as she was passed from orphanage to orphanage.

Mayor Coldstone wiped his hand across his face and paused for a moment as he regained his frigid, stern expression. He was intent on finishing this spectacle. He took a deep breath then firmly roared in a fearsome, escalating voice, "Christmas is not real. Santa is not real and your Humbugs are not real!"

The villagers looked at each other in dismay. Doubt crossed their minds. Each wondered if the humming they had heard had been real. They started talking and doubting and fear crept in. In their minds they questioned themselves. *Do the others think I'm foolish? How could I have believed? I've never heard of something so absurd.* As they looked at each other the doubts increased. As they talked and doubted, they agreed it was foolish. The idea so ridiculous some even laughed. How could they have believed something so far-fetched?

"Stop!" exclaimed Mayor Coldstone. Silence again. "Listen. It is gone." Everyone listened and the hum was gone. Even Mimi could not hear the Humbugs. Mayor Coldstone looked down at Mimi and scoffed, "Silly girl, I don't want to hear your voice ever again!" With that he briskly walked through the the crowd and out the door. All the villagers looked down at Mimi with disdain.

"None of you believe?" questioned Mimi as tears streamed down her face. Faces, cold again, turned away and made their way to the door. Mrs. Sleet took Mimi's hand and pulled her across the hall. As Mimi stepped out the door, the face of Charlie Chapman blurred through her tears. Charlie stood next to his father, whose expression was cold and stern. Charlie watched as Mimi's tears turned to ice and shattered on the floor.

Humbug

Chester Chapman pulled his son onto the cold winter streets and quickly a sheet of ice formed on his cheeks. Silence returned to the freezing winter town and ice again formed on the villagers faces.

Charlie looked around at the faces and a tear rolled down his cheek, it too froze, fell to the ground and shattered. Something happened that moment. His heart caught fire inside his chest. He felt a pounding determination to do something he had never done. A smile erupted on his face and he pulled his hand from his father's grasp and ran the other way.

Chester Chapman, shocked, turned to see Charlie slide around a corner. Charlie sprinted all the way to the orphanage and burst through the door.

In the attic Mimi sat alone crying. The warmth had left her and her cheeks were lined with frozen tears. The hatch flew open as Charlie entered the attic. Mimi turned with a start then calmed herself. More tears rolled down her cheeks. "He can't hum anymore," said Mimi as the tears froze to her face. Mimi held out her hand and in it was the small green bug. The Humbug opened its mouth and nothing was there. It looked around confused and sadly put its hands over its mouth.

"That's your Humbug?" questioned Charlie.

Mimi nodded, still crying.

"I believe you, Mimi," Charlie said with a smile, "and I believe in your Humbug."

"You do?" Mimi looked at Charlie and his glow was contagious. The ice on her cheeks melted as her smile came back. Warmth flowed through her heart, "Thank you."

Humbug

Just then the Humbug looked up at Mimi and Charlie and opened its mouth. It was very quiet at first but soon became audible. From the tiny mouth came a beautiful hum. The Humbug jumped from Mimi's hand and flew to the window.

"He is wonderful," said Charlie.

Several bugs came out of hiding in the attic and started to hum with Mimi's Humbug. The chorus swelled and soon children from all over the orphanage climbed into the attic. Smiles came across the faces of all the children and they began singing with the Humbugs. A Christmas chorus echoed throughout the town.

The villagers came out from their houses and crowded into the streets. Charlie opened the window to the attic and the people listened with curiosity.

Mrs. Sleet crawled up through the hatch. Her frozen face softened as she saw the Humbugs and the children singing. She choked for a moment then softly said, "Humbugs?" Mimi nodded and smiled.

Bells were then heard in the distance. Questioningly, Mrs. Sleet asked, "Humbells?"

Mimi ran to the window, "No, much better!"

From the top of the mountain the bells rang louder. The sound got bolder and stronger and stronger. Suddenly over the crest of the mountain nine reindeer, one with a red nose, burst forth with a glowing red sleigh. "Ho, Ho, Ho, merry Christmas!"

The sleigh swooped over the village and the crowd watched in awe. The warm magical wind from the sleigh blew the frost off the Mayor's face and he smiled. "Santa?" said the Mayor.

"Merry Christmas, Winterton!" Santa cheerfully said with a grin.

anta's sleigh and reindeer again swooped over the crowd then landed on the roof of the orphanage. Santa rolled from his sleigh and walked to the window where he leaned down to two bright smiling children and an astonished Mrs. Sleet. "Mimi and Charlie, thank you for believing." He then put his hand out and several Humbugs stepped onto his mitten. "I haven't been to this village in over a hundred years. Thank you for humming. I need more Humbugs like you."

Santa turned to the crowd and said, "Merry Christmas, Winterton!" He then smiled and rushed to his sleigh. "Ho, Ho, Ho, Merry Christmas!" The sleigh swooped into the air." Merry Christmas to all and have a wonderful night, keep your Humbugs humming when you turn out the light!" With that he soared over the mountain and disappeared.

The villagers stood still, but this time with warm delight and a chorus of humming swelled from orphange small window above. Several Humbugs had gathered and wore scarves, hats and gloves. Their humming was cheerful and filled with love. The villagers smiled and joined in the song as more Humbugs chimed in from other windows above.

The humming continued long into the night. People were smiling and hugging and singing – the feelings were warm and gentle and pleasing. A beautiful result of that magical night is that the warmth continued every night. Christmases come and Christmases go, but the good feelings and the giving continue to grow. Since that day there has not been one cold season, the Humbugs still hum and Christmas love is the reason.

THE END